The Game

Sean McDermott

chipmunkapublishing
the mental health publisher

Published by
Chipmunkapublishing
PO Box 6872
Brentwood
Essex CM13 1ZT
United Kingdom

http://www.chipmunkapublishing.com

Copyright © Sean McDermott 2012

Edited by Lesley Kirk

ISBN   978-1-84991-818-3

Chipmunkapublishing   gratefully   acknowledge   the support of Arts Council England.

INTRODUCTION

From an early age I always found it hard to accept that there wasn't more to life than the average daily grind. By the age of 15 however I started hanging around with friends and looking up to rock stars as role models. They smoked a lot of marijuana so we did too and it seemed OK, but around the same time I lost interest in school - partly because I wanted to learn things for myself rather than just copy from text books but partly because I didn't want to go. The only subject that ever really held my interest was Sociology.

In 1990 things spiralled out of control. I was admitted to a psychiatric hospital and spent the next few years experiencing the many facets of the mental health system. The environment was often unsuitable for recovery and some of the staff was unhelpful. Some of them were very helpful though and as time went on I realised that people in positions of authority weren't all bad.

I didn't find working life easy when I tried to get into it as people were often unkind to me but during one of my stays in hospital I picked up my guitar and rediscovered my creativity. I started writing poems and songs and this is something I've continued ever since. During this process I have learned much about myself, about people in general and the nature of the world we live in. Ironically, if I hadn't become ill I'm not sure if this would have happened, so in a way things have come full circle and I've realised that it's OK to be part of society and still retain a level of individuality. I'm now trying to get voluntary work and have started giving talks and readings about my experiences. I hope you will gain something from this.

Sean McDermott 2011

CONTENTS

The Game

Relics

Worlds fall into myths,
past years into the mist,
dust rises
and blows away

ghost towns, relics
to be seen or preserved
from times that were hard
in other worlds.

Can I ask you to imagine…….

…living in somebody else's 9 to 5 workplace?

Can you imagine doors are banging very loudly –
so much so you want to become deaf?

Can you imagine you're tired and you can't get to
sleep?

Can you imagine being given relaxants in an
environment which is tormenting you?

Can you imagine wanting to sleep and being kept
awake?

Can you imagine not being able to offer your
visitors anything?

Can you imagine being very, very frightened and
no-one understands that your fear is real?

Can you imagine being given pills to recover from a
terrifying experience?

Can you imagine being shaped into something
which is contrary to who you are?

Can you imagine being so completely on your own
you feel dead?

Can you imagine then being told you will never get
better?

Blind Utopia

The sun shines through the window
and dances on the floor,
just another reason for drugs to score
and then when it's over you want more,
enticing you into a world unreal
so that you're not even sure how you feel,
the dream ends and reality is so cold
but you can't say you were never told.

Trap

Social control goes too far, living for money and car,
stifling freedom for the sake of the state,
if you want happiness you'll have to wait,
endless production, spiralling wealth -
a trap destroying your mental health,
get up in the morning, the same day awaits,
keeping appointments and dates,
monotony of thoughts like a machine made by man
but you must earn a wage if you can.
Things that differ cannot be seen and true,
because of the blind things we do.

Jim Morrison

Spiritual son of a rock n roll man,

you know he does the best he can,

he brought your soul when you tossed the dice

to live in sweet dreams, a paradise,

rock on son, rock on,

desire is sweet and so is your song

but you beg for your soul to return,

as a passion burns.

Black File

Life written down to help this one in need,
like a bad school report, never freed.
They get away with what they like,
adult school children picking for a fight,
authority gives them reason to justify what they do
whilst too many lives are dead and through.

The Change

Play the game and win?

Change and fit in?

It's no lie like you once thought

in a society where freedom is bought.

Get the best even if it's wrong?

Make your mark and then belong?

So much bad, so much good,

but you would change it if you could.

Anger

Anger was my friend on the ward,

eyes like weapons and a heart burning cold,

exploding minds as rules were told

but he was my friend with a heart of gold.

We are all fuelled with fire until the soul dies.

Why did no-one hear his cries?

Solitude

Inside walls of brick,

alone and sick,

the clock ticks the time away,

I can't feel better, no matter what they say,

stricken with a burden and I don't know why,

all that's left is for me to try

to look at the good all around;

a positive outlook can be found.

The Evil Game

Sex, crime and drugs – a playground for thugs,

once you're sucked in, that's when the pain begins,

addiction takes control and time takes its toll,

giving you nothing for your life has gone,

take the guitar and play a song,

it sounds good so you get strong,

forget the past and you'll live long.

The End Will Come

Man claims superiority over all things
but bad news to the earth he brings,
the sun shines and the bird sings
yet what is intelligence and what has it done –
nothing if only war has come,
awe and wonder destroyed day by day,
trees and grass burnt away
and still man has the last say.

Swans

Swans elegant and sincere
add to the lake's atmosphere,
water crystal clear,
animals close and dear,
the onlooker sheds a tear
for this is the final home –
polluted, disregarded;
an everyday tomb.

The Game

Emotions wounded by life's jagged edge,

souls sold for evil carnage,

Utopia cast aside as a childish dream,

books and files tell us where we have been,

but if you are vigilant in what you believe,

twisting the chains of the life you lead

you can break the bonds and leave.

Another Chance

The ideal world I wish to see,

my thoughts tell me

it's not to be.

Where do they come from?

And what do they know?

How to nurture a

mind and grow?

Sleepy eyes disguise

what's within,

come on son, carry on

and don't give in,

your soul is tired

and your body is thin

but you must try again

and this time win.

Recovery

You don't know what's right and wrong,

you've lost the plot and you don't belong,

kindness and compassion can cure your mind

and then reality you can find,

the life around you will help –

you're more than a medical cure

so believe me when I say

there will soon be a brighter day.

Day Off

The worker moans a groan

for today he wants to stay at home,

not cutting and grinding stone.

Will he be better lazing round doing nowt?

Or going fishing and catching trout?

Is this what his life is about?

Or will he be labelled a lout?

Beat the Cycle

Opinions about a rightful decision
can build on ideas with precision,
expanding on thoughts, feelings and emotion
will break the cycle of monotonous motion,
freedom of thought cannot be bought,
but breaking down the logical restraint
dissolves the boundaries to create.

The Offshore Journey

The wind blows into the sails fast and quick,

the sailors are skilled and slick,

endurance becomes the main factor,

the sun is the reactor,

needing to see the final goal

as they bet the dice they roll,

will they win, will they lose

and on the waves have a smooth cruise?

The Fountain of Life

Eyes as bright as sparkling water

reflected into my mind,

summer days in childlike ways

you were so kind,

fountains that flowed so free

and all the birds

singing in the trees

like a beautiful, timeless dream,

I gave it to you

and all of our wishes came true.

Fool's Gold?

Stones caressed by the sea,

for jewels they were meant to be,

sparkling in the hands of the

rich and poor, but we

don't know what they're for.

How still the light shines

in patterns and rhymes,

those don't need reasons in time.

The End of the Race

Some are rich, some are poor,
some make love, some make war,
what are the reasons for life to endure?
Is it just for boredom to cure?
Better or worse is a competitive curse
but if you climb up the scale of respect
you'll have no need to look back, regret.

Strange World

Overwhelmed by the wonders of

creation, not listening to the laws

of restriction,

the hierarchies,

dictation,

competitive

affliction,

drawn into a world where you don't fit in,

higher or lower you can't win

but being equal is no sin.

Journey

Rugged is the path of the hardened soul

not needing any ambition or goal,

pacing himself as the path goes steeper,

waiting to meet the midnight creeper;

angel of life, angel of death

competing with God's wrath inside his mind,

all of this you may find

but in the end you'll know He is kind.

Spark of Hope

A ray of light
cuts through the night
like a shooting star,
cool, like a reflection
you can touch,
dissolving the darkness
captured in the mind,
a purer perception
so bright it could
almost blind.

The Riddle

Today I will rest and think about me
because there are things I would clearly see
if I were left alone to be.
I thought things would always be the same
with information in my brain –
there to protect me and keep me sane.
choosing to forget the game.

The Call of Life

Colours radiant and bright,
silence in the still of night
like a new life, born into light,
I've given up the daily fight
and truth calls me sincere
into this new way where
the mind is clear.

Sean Mcdermott

Water

Ebbing peace into my soul,

ripples so calm and sweet,

essence of life, of grace, of flow,

a force that never dies,

it has

no good,

no bad,

no lies.

Transition to Reality

What I am thinking might not be real,
explaining the way I don't want to feel,
answers might come warm and kind
for a taste of reality I could find,
positive ideas real and true
give me reasons for things to do,
give me freedom to a way unknown,
out of the illness I have grown,
so thank the world and God above
we all can still believe in love.

Rainbow River

Rainbow of wishes,

river of fishes,

radiant in colour,

needing protection against forces

that could make them duller,

factories pumping blackness

far from the human eye

so that we can't see the fish that die,

but the end of the story is good indeed

if we think of the fish in need,

given a new home to swim and breed.

Compassion for the Text Book

Helping the ill is very serious,

the doses are high and you're delirious,

text book examinations teach about realizations,

chemical alterations and verbal interventions

but compassion like children we all need

when we feel like our minds bleed,

the blood of tuition, leading to fruition

as new as the morning sun,

the battle of insanity is won.

New Life

When death no longer exists
and life is given the final kiss
living is external bliss,
the spiritual world talks from the other side,
relating to people with music helps you confide,
not to be done in life for one day you will depart
and then on a magical journey you will start.

Getting Better

If you're feeling dead
and there are too many thoughts in your head
don't forget there is always someone who will call
on you

getting better day by day
getting better day by day.

If you're feeling low and you've got nowhere to go
there is one thing you should know
we love you so, we love you so

getting better day by day
getting better day by day.

Find a friend and talk things through,
the past is gone, the future's new,
there is always something you can do

getting better day by day
getting better in your own way.

Born Again

Death comes sudden and swift,

on the angels' wings you drift,

for when the time is right

you will be born into the light

to forget the past like a sudden blow

and watch the sun eternally glow.

New Way

Everybody plays a part and changes

the destiny of what is to come,

take time to know what's needed

and what is to be done.

Is it written what will be

in years far ahead?

Not believing what they think

or what is being said?

How can we know as things are

different, changing day by day

and if things are different

you can find your own – new way.

Reviews of Sean McDermott's 'The Game'

'The poetry of Sean is like no other, reading them is like stripping away the meaningless things of life. They talk in a fashion that could be described as both wise and child like. They deal with emotionally charged issues that are often ignored. They make us contemplate society as a whole and question where our own purity and innocence has gone. Perhaps it takes a naïve view from a pure yet troubled mind to show us the way forward? The work is strengthened by both the beautifully coloured imagery that Sean uses and the sadness and joy that dance together through them.'

Bob Malpiedi,

Manager, Newcastle and Gateshead Art Studio

'Sean's collection of poems captures a tale of recovery, intensely personal but with universal appeal and application. His work has a deceptive simplicity, conveying deep emotions and complex situations in a pithy, accessible fashion. He never shies away from asking the obvious but difficult questions about life, those which too many prefer not to consider because of the soul-searching that would entail. His honesty and openness are a credit to him, and shine through in his poems; recommended reading.'

Alisdair Cameron,

Launchpad Team Leader

www.ingramcontent.com/pod-product-compliance
Lightning Source LLC
Chambersburg PA
CBHW031142270326
41931CB00007B/655